JOURNEY INTO INNER SPACE

FIND YOUR TRUE SELF

A BRAHMA KUMARIS PRODUCTION

JOURNEY INTO INNER SPACE

FIND YOUR TRUE SELF

A BRAHMA KUMARIS PRODUCTION

 BKIS

Journey Into Inner Space
Find Your True Self

A Brahma Kumaris Production
Commentary by Clarke Peters
Meditation by Sister Jayanti`
Posters by Cécile Cayla Boucharel
Animations by Godlywood Studios and Al Hodgson
Augmented Reality by Al Hodgson
Text by Neville Hodgkinson and Cécile Cayla Boucharel

ISBN Number: 978-1-912187-00-3

First Edition 2019

Published by Brahma Kumaris Information Services Ltd.,
in association with Brahma Kumaris World Spiritual University (UK)
Registered Charity No. 269971.
Global Co-operation House, 65 Pound Lane, London NW10 2HH, UK

Cover and book lay out by Judi Rich, Canada
Printed by CPI Digital Printers, UK

www.inspiredstillness.com
email: hello@inspiredstillness.com
www.brahmakumaris.org

INTRODUCTION

This book teams discoveries from the frontiers of science with ancient and modern wisdom to offer an explanation of what is meant by the inner life, the world of the spirit or soul, as compared with the physical world around us.

It combines images and text to lead you on an experiential journey into your own "inner space", using a novel technology called Augmented Reality. You can take the journey wherever you are, using a smartphone or tablet.

Just download Zappar free from your app store, scan the zappcode beside each image, aim at the whole image and see it come to life.

Work your way through from images one to eight. Step by step, you'll hear the renowned actor and director Clarke Peters narrate the essence of new understandings linking science and spirit, giving us a glimpse of our divinity. Each commentary, lasting about one minute, is amplified in the book's text, with detailed background information and references.

The journey ends — and also, in a way, begins — with a meditation led by Sister Jayanti, one of the world's most experienced teachers of Raja Yoga. You can listen to her gently guiding each one of us towards our own, personal inner space in the audio accompanying image number nine.

When we enter this space, we become aware of a quite different environment from the usual one presented to us by our senses. It's a unique space inside each one of us, inaccessible to others, and yet a place where we connect to a feeling and understanding of being part of a bigger picture than we normally experience.

It can be as fascinating and energising as the outside world, if not more so.

But it is not an opting out. By entering this inner space we gain access to wisdom and insights that help us to understand ourselves, each other, and the world around us. And we discover that if we learn to keep this awareness with us, even as we negotiate everyday life, we greatly increase our ability to live constructively and well.

Enjoy the journey!

CONTENTS

THE JOURNEY

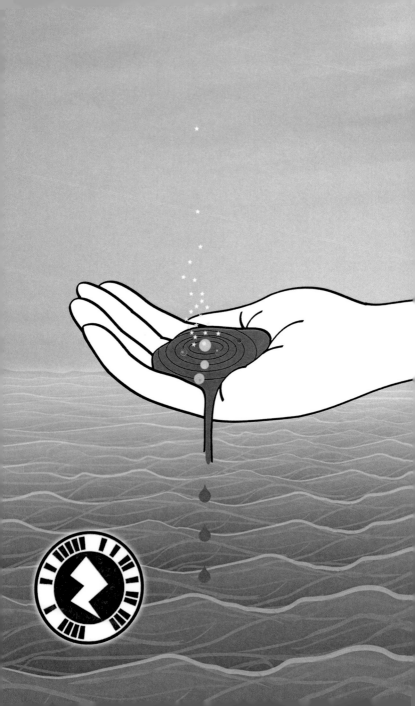

STEP ONE: A NEW STORY

A mini-solar system turns, linked to a vibrational sea and a region of subtle light

A new story is emerging about the nature of the universe we inhabit. It attributes a fundamental role to consciousness or spirit in creating as well as experiencing the physical world.

The Cosmic Hologram[1], by cosmologist and physicist Jude Currivan, states: "Everything that manifests in the physical world emerges from deeper and ordered levels of non-physical and in-formed reality." It is as if Nature has an intelligence of her own, and the true ground of our individual being lies within this common consciousness.

This new story builds on discoveries made nearly a century ago by the pioneers of quantum mechanics, a branch of physics that emerged from studies of the behaviour of elementary particles.

---

[1] *The Cosmic Hologram – In-formation at the Centre of Creation*, by Jude Currivan (Inner Traditions, Rochester, Vermont, 2017)

Max Planck (1858-1947), a German physicist, was first to develop the idea of the quantum when he saw that energy is exchanged not continuously, but in finite bits, or "quanta".

His explorations led him to a momentous conclusion: "As a man who has devoted his whole life to the most clearheaded science, to the study of matter, I can tell you as a result of my research about the atoms this much: there is no matter as such!

"All matter originates and exists only by virtue of a force which brings the particles of an atom to vibration and holds this most minute solar system of the atom together...We must assume behind this force the existence of a conscious and intelligent spirit. This spirit is the matrix of all matter."

Sir James Jeans, an English astrophysicist, also famously concluded in his 1930 book *The Mysterious Universe*: "The stream of knowledge is heading towards a non-mechanical reality; the universe begins to look more like a great thought than like a great machine. Mind no longer appears to be an accidental intruder into the realm of matter...we ought rather hail it as the creator and governor of the realm of matter."

These revolutionary ideas from within the world of science informed and encouraged spiritual researchers of that era. The idea of a cosmic mind was explored in many of the books of Paul Brunton[2], for example, who studied ancient sacred texts and interviewed numerous wisdom teachers of the East in the 1930s and 40s. Summarising his findings, he wrote: "Life has planted us in a universe of thoughts, whereas we have taken it to be a universe of matter."

Today, the practical benefits of quantum technologies are all around us. Thanks to an understanding of the quantum laws, the latest generations of microprocessors contain billions of transistors.

For decades, however, as a society we have shown a reluctance to face the implications of quantum theory for our understanding of mind and spirit. The possibility that consciousness is fundamental – and that the material universe derives from consciousness, not consciousness from the material universe – largely disappeared from view.

Perhaps partly in revulsion against the horrors wrought in the name of Nazi and Stalinist ideologies, post-war generations tended to be determinedly down-to-earth.

---

[2] See: http://www.paulbrunton.org/

3

Material prosperity became a near-universal goal, and even the transcendental insights at the roots of long-established religions tended to be overlooked or forgotten.

Now, that is changing.

STEP TWO: WHO WE ARE

Physical forms, including the body, manifest in our awareness through interactions in vibrational fields

Science is offering us an amplified picture of reality. It calls on us to rethink who we are and where we have come from.

Mathematicians, physicists, astronomers, brain scientists and others are advancing the frontiers of a new, post-materialist science, pointing to a mind-like quality at the root of existence.[3]

In this understanding, "things" – such as bodies, and germs, and trees, and galaxies – manifest in our awareness through subtle vibrational fields which carry a vast matrix of information.

Ervin Laszlo, a Hungarian polymath and philosopher of science writes: "There is a new concept of what the

---

[3] See: http://opensciences.org/about/manifesto-for-a-post-materialist-science and also https://www.frontiersin.org/articles/10.3389/fnhum.2014.00017/full

world truly is. It is not an ensemble of separate bits of matter moving in accordance with mechanistic laws, but an intrinsically whole system where all things are connected in ways that transcend the previously known laws of space and time."[4]

If the universe shows intelligence, working as an integrated system rather than a giant machine, who or what lies behind that system, and keeps it running?

A theory developed by Donald Hoffman, professor of cognitive science at the University of California at Irvine, USA, argues that "conscious agents" comprise the deepest reality. The world, he suggests, consists entirely of these agents (which include human beings) and their experiences.

The objects that seem so real to us when presented to our senses are actually like icons on a computer desktop – a useful guide to how we need to act, but not reality itself.

"Consciousness...is not a latecomer in the evolutionary history of the universe, arising from complex interactions of unconscious matter and fields," he writes. "Consciousness is first; matter and fields depend on it for their very existence."[5]

---

[4] *The Intelligence of the Cosmos: Why Are We Here*, Inner Traditions, Rochester, USA, 2017

[5] In *Conscious Realism and the Mind-Body Problem*, Donald D. Hoffman (2008), *Mind & Matter* Vol. 6(1), pp 87-121

Experimental results support these extraordinary ideas. They indicate that the everyday world we perceive is not something "out there", independent of consciousness.[6]

This doesn't mean that the world is merely one's own personal hallucination or act of imagination. Rather, the mind of nature that underlies the world is transpersonal – it far transcends any individual psyche. And it behaves according to natural laws, so this new understanding would not mean the end of traditional science.

But how we think about ourselves - and death - would be transformed. "If mind is generated by the brain, then it's over when the brain decomposes when you die," says artificial intelligence expert Bernardo Kastrup. With the new thinking, "when the brain decomposes, the mind is free."

The idea is gaining ground of the brain as a kind of filter, a construct of consciousness enabling us to get an individual "take" on the world so as to manage ourselves in the game of life. This means that whilst all of us have a brain, we are not our brains, as author Deepak Chopra and neurologist Rudolf Tanzi have argued.[7]

---

[6] See article posted in *Scientific American*, 29 May, 2018, by Bernardo Kastrup, Dutch computer engineer and specialist in artificial intelligence; Henry P. Stapp, theoretical physicist, University of California Lawrence Berkeley Laboratory, specialising in quantum theory; and Menas Kafatos, Professor of Computational Physics, Chapman University, USA.

[7] https://www.huffingtonpost.com/deepak-chopra/mind-brain_b_1379446.html.

The Italian theoretical physicist Carlo Rovelli, author of the best-selling *Seven Brief Lessons on Physics, and Reality Is Not What It Seems*[8], eloquently describes strides made in 21st-century science towards obtaining a picture of the fundamental structure of the physical world. This picture emerges from a field of study called quantum gravity, which seeks to reconcile quantum theory with what Einstein's relativity theory tells us about gravity.

Rovelli, like many of his colleagues, dismisses the concept of "soul" as a primary entity distinct from the body. "There is not an 'I' and 'the neurons in my brain'," he declares. "They are the same thing...I am my body, and what happens in my brain and heart, with their immense and, for me, inextricable complexity."

But the picture he paints of the quantum world does not seem far from that described in the new story.[9]

He writes: "It is a world which does not exist in space and does not develop in time. A world made up solely of interacting quantum fields, the swarming of which generates – through a dense network of reciprocal interactions – space, time, particles, waves and light."

---

[8] Both published by Penguin Random House UK

[9] See also *You Are the Universe – Discovering Your Cosmic Self* and *Why It Matters,* Deepak Chopra and Menas Kafatos, Harmony Books, 2017

Could it be that even this world of interacting fields is "not what it seems", because even this is not reality itself? That this is a mental universe, and that you and I are among the "conscious agents" who both put on and experience the show?

STEP THREE:
DEATH IS NOT THE END

Flowers bloom, and fade away...the physical world is in constant movement, but is there more to life than matter?

Whereas bodies turn to dust, souls are eternal. This glorious truth becomes hidden when we get lost in the physical aspects of existence.

For centuries, an awareness of the divine was never far from people's minds. Theologians, philosophers and artists differed in their views on what might happen between this life and the next, but the idea of an immortal soul was largely unquestioned.

Today, many people see that idea as an outdated superstition. Science has been so successful in helping to make our lives more comfortable that we tend to believe the physical world is all there is. Evolutionary principles seemed enough to explain the wonder and complexity of life.

But a growing weight of evidence supports the idea that the core of our being is not only non-physical, but eternal transcending time and space.

People brought back from clinical death or deep coma often report heightened mental functions while their brain activity was absent or impaired. Long-term studies of such cases have convinced previously sceptical investigators that consciousness not merely continues after death, but in a greatly expanded form. The subjects of these so-called Near-Death Experiences (NDE) seem to become part of what the visionary writer Aldous Huxley called "mind-at large". At the same time, they keep a sense of individuality.

Pim Van Lommel, a Dutch cardiologist, led a 10-year study interviewing hundreds of patients revived after a cardiac arrest. Many of the subjects were transformed, he said "by the conscious experience of a dimension where time and distance play no role, where past and future can be glimpsed, where they feel complete and healed, and where they can experience unlimited wisdom and unconditional love...People realise that death is not the end.

"Enveloped by light, people experience total acceptance

and unconditional love and have access to a deep knowledge and wisdom, with indescribable clarity and insight."

Van Lommel found that just over a fifth of the patients in his study reported an ongoing experience after the medical monitors had pronounced them dead. The results were first published in *The Lancet,* a British medical journal, then in *Consciousness Beyond Life – The Science of the Near-Death Experience*[10], a book combining the stories of many patients with an exploration of the new scientific thinking within which their accounts make sense.

The patients described their experiences like this:

"It seemed as if time and distance didn't exist. I was everywhere at once, and sometimes my attention was focused on something and I was there too."

"The pinnacle of everything there is, of energy, of love especially, of warmth, of beauty."

"I can live without my body, but apparently my body cannot live without me."

"My NDE has transformed my emotions...everything I do

---

[10] HarperCollins, 2010

now is aimed at reliving and spreading this feeling of love."

"I asked if God was the light, and the answer was: 'No, God is not the light, the light is what happens when God breathes'."

"I think death is a really nasty, bad lie."

The study included long-term follow-up, and Van Lommel found that as well as a huge decrease in fear of death reported by the subjects immediately after the NDE, their fear decreased even further over the years.

Questions remain. If there is a deep awareness common to us all, independent of the brain, why is it not reported more often among patients who recover from periods of unconsciousness bordering on death? Almost four fifths of the subjects in Van Lommel's study did not report an NDE.

The answer may be that all such patients do have these experiences, but not all recall them. "Consciousness may never be absent," Bernardo Kastrup writes. "What we refer to as periods of unconsciousness, be they sleep, anaesthesia, or fainting, may be reinterpreted as periods in which memory formation is impaired."[11]

In his best-selling book *Proof of Heaven*,[12] Eben Alexander, an eminent neurosurgeon, describes his recollections of a week-long coma caused by a rare form of bacterial meningitis. "I was encountering the reality of a world of consciousness that existed completely free of the limitations of my physical brain", he says.

He felt desperate to communicate what he had learned as soon as he recovered his everyday faculties. Love and compassion, he writes, "are far more than the abstractions many of us believe them to be. They are real. They are concrete. And they make up the very fabric of the spiritual realm.

"Love is, without a doubt, the basis of everything...the reality of realities, the incomprehensibly glorious truth of truths that lives and breathes at the core of everything that exists or that ever will exist, and no remotely accurate understanding of who and what we are can be achieved by anyone who does not know it, and embody it in all their actions. We have the ability to recover our connection with that idyllic realm."

Dr Jill Bolte Taylor, a brain scientist who suffered a

---

[11] http://www.skeptiko.com/bernardo-kastrup-consciousness-research/
[12] Piatkus, 2012

haemorrhage in her own brain's left hemisphere, also on recovery, felt a passion to communicate the expanded consciousness and connectedness she felt as she lost her normal faculties. She describes the experience in her book *My Stroke of Insight*[13] and in a dramatic talk in which she recalls feeling: "I am the life-force power of the universe. I am the life-force power of the 50 trillion beautiful molecular geniuses that make up my form, at one with all that is."[14]

In similar vein, Anita Moorjani has related in her book *Dying To Be Me*[15], and also in a TED talk[16], how she went into a state of super-awareness during a coma brought on by end-stage lymphoma. "It felt as though I had 360 degree peripheral vision...It was as if I had expanded beyond my body," she says. "I was aware of my physical body – I could see it lying there on the hospital bed – but I was no longer attached to that body. It felt as though I could be everywhere at the same time. Wherever I put my awareness, there I was."

She felt as though connected to everybody, including the doctors and nurses as well as relatives. "When we're not expressing in our physical bodies, you and I and all of us

---

[13] Penguin Books, USA, 2008

[14] https://www.ted.com/talks/jill_bolte_taylor_s_powerful_stroke_of_insight?language=en

[15] Hay House, 2012

[16] https://www.youtube.com/watch?v=rhcJNJbRJ6U

are expressions of the same consciousness. That's what it felt like."

On regaining consciousness, she improved so rapidly that she left hospital within weeks. The cancer, which she had fought for four years, disappeared completely.

As with so many others who have gone beyond the brain in this way, her life was never to be the same again. Moorjani puts it like this:

Imagine that we are in a totally darkened warehouse, that's pitch black. You can't see anything. But in your hand, you hold a little flashlight, with which you navigate your way through the dark. Everything you see in the warehouse is only what you see with the beam of the flashlight.

Imagine one day, big floodlights go on, so the whole warehouse is illuminated, and you realise it's huge, and lined with shelves and shelves and shelves of all kinds of different things. Imagine the lights go off again. Although all you can see is from the beam of the one flashlight, at least you now know there is so much more that exists simultaneously and alongside the things that you can see. The beam of the flashlight is your awareness. It becomes your reality, what you experience. We would have a very different world if we changed our awareness.

We don't have to die, or even come close to physical death, in order to see and know more of that light – to expand our awareness beyond the limitations of our conditioned brain-based sense of self.

It requires putting aside our self-centredness – our ego – and gradually facing up to and removing the false beliefs we hold, that obscure the light of pure consciousness within.

This understanding lies behind the enduring greatness of the work of C.S. Lewis, an Oxford don who transformed from atheist to committed Christian. In his classic book series *Chronicles of Narnia,* he wrote: "Give up yourself and you'll find your real self. Lose your life and you'll save it. Submit to death, submit with every fibre of your being and you'll find eternal life."

it is raining

it is raining

STEP FOUR:
SCIENCE AND SILENCE

*"Silent raindrops fall" when,
like Simon and Garfunkel,
we listen to the sound of silence*

What does "the sound of silence" mean? It seems paradoxical.

When we still the mind through meditation, contemplation or prayer, and free the self from the brain's habitual chatter, a different sound is heard inside. It is the sound of a deeper understanding and experience of ourselves and the world around us.

The popular hymn "Dear Lord and Father of Mankind", based on a poem by American Quaker John Whittier, conveys this understanding:

*Drop Thy still dews of quietness,
Till all our strivings cease;
Take from our souls the strain and stress,*

And let our ordered lives confess
The beauty of Thy peace.

In silence, we are approaching territory often described by poets and mystics.

Mother Julian of Norwich, a 14th-century English mystic who lived in isolation for much of her life, discovered "a force of love moving through the universe that holds us fast, and will never let us go." She wrote about it in her *Revelations of Divine Love*, the first book in the English language written by a woman.

Julian experienced an overwhelming sense of peace at the peak of an illness in which she almost died. It left her with an absolute conviction as to the ultimate benevolence of creation. A song based on her teachings contains the lines

All shall be well,
I'm telling you.
Let winter come and go
All shall be well again, I know.

A similar sense of a benign and subtle energy at work within Nature is conveyed by William Wordsworth in his *Lines*

Composed a Few Miles above Tintern Abbey:

> *...And I have felt*
> *A presence that disturbs me with the joy*
> *Of elevated thoughts; a sense sublime*
> *Of something far more deeply infused,*
> *Whose dwelling is the light of the setting suns,*
> *And the round ocean and the living air,*
> *And the blue sky, and in the mind of man.*
> *A motion and a spirit, that impels*
> *All thinking things, all objects of all thought,*
> *And rolls through all things.*

John Keats's *On Death* also invites us to realise an awakened state of being that lies behind the "dream" of life:

> *Can death be sleep, when life is but a dream.*
> *And scenes of bliss pass as a phantom by?*
> *The transient pleasures as a vision seem,*
> *And yet we think the greatest pain's to die.*
>
> *How strange it is that man on earth should roam,*
> *And lead a life of woe, but not forsake*
> *His rugged path; nor dare he view alone*
> *His future doom which is but to awake.*

In similar vein, Shakespeare wrote:

Thou hast nor youth nor age,
But, as it were, an after-dinner's sleep, dreaming on both.

The question arises, who — or what — is this "dreamer"?

After centuries in which science and spirituality have seemed to give sharply contrasting views, a scientific answer may at last be emerging.

Physicist Amit Goswami, who has spent decades examining the meaning of quantum theory for our understanding of ourselves,[17] says the mysteries thrown up by the theory disappear when we understand that consciousness itself creates the world that manifests around us.

He describes this consciousness as unitive, meaning it unfolds just one script, of a divine play. We are all beings of consciousness within the play, enacting our individual parts moment by moment. But there are underlying threads that ensure cohesion and purpose. We are co-creators of the material world, unique and self-contained, yet connected to the whole.

---

[17] See *The Visionary Window – A Quantum Physicist's Guide to Enlightenment*, Quest Books, 2000, and *The Self-Aware Universe – How Consciousness Creates the Material World*, Simon and Schuster, 1993

This helps us to understand what is happening when we turn our attention inwards, towards an awareness of the inner being. Prayer, and meditation, bring a sense of joy, and replenishment, when they enable us to feel connected to a source of universal wisdom.

The true spiritual journey within leads us from our limited, everyday identities towards the joy of self-transcendence, and an increasing sense of alignment to a higher power.

The sound of silence is the sound of that inner power being replenished, or expressed. It's not a passive state. It means both receiving a positive energy, through connecting with inner truth, and emerging it through our actions and relationships.

There are many ways to access this energy other than withdrawal and solitude. Places of worship; uplifting music; works of art that touch the soul and take you out of the "ego tunnel" into a wider sense of reality; mountains and other high places that expand your consciousness, as well your vision; even the comradeship of a shared task or goal - all these are ways of charging the battery of our wellbeing.

In all those examples, however, there is an element of ou
depending on whatever is going on outside of us. As we g
deeper inside, we can glimpse total freedom

STEP FIVE:
BREAKING THE SPELL

Ignorance pulled us into pieces.
Contemplating eternal truths makes us well again.

The growth of interest in all types of meditation, and other reflective practices, is a sign of our need to restore balance between our inner and outer worlds.

We are happiest when expressing positive attributes such as kindness and wisdom, and seeing those qualities in the lives of others.

But today the currency of kindness is in increasingly short supply. When this is reflected in our actions, much suffering results.

An over-demanding ego makes us chase after illusory goals, of name or fame. If we meet those goals, the ego grows bigger and demands more. Then, to meet those fresh demands, we may find ourselves hardening our hearts to the harm we are causing to others, as well as to ourselves.

When we fail to meet these ever-increasing expectations, a
ultimately we must, a painful breakdown in our self-respec
is likely, perhaps accompanied by a heart attack or othe
catastrophic illness.

The animal kingdom, and even the elements, are als
greatly troubled by the human condition. Millions o
sentient creatures suffer every day within an often heartles
system of industrialised food production. The planet, it
atmosphere and eco-systems are groaning under the weigh
of our relentless drive for economic growth and greate
prosperity.

Many remain largely oblivious to the harm we are causing
It is as though we are under a spell of forgetfulness. Yet th
longing – and the need – to know the deeper, transformativ
dimension of reality is becoming more and more apparent

The global success of J.K. Rowling's Harry Potter storie
is a sign of this need. At Hogwarts School of Witchcraf
and Wizardry, Harry learns about the power of the minc
– and most importantly, how it can be used for both goo
and ill. Love eventually proves more powerful than th
dark forces. To restore the ability to live fully by that love

Harry, Hermione and Ron have to undergo many tests with determination and courage – and ultimately, as C.S. Lewis realised, to face death.

How can we begin to break the spell that has caused our true nature to become forgotten?

The American author Jack Kornfield, who trained as a Buddhist monk and has been one of the key teachers bringing mindfulness practice to the West, says that sometimes the opening of the mind and heart "comes as a call from the gods, a pull from outside of our ordinary life... Over and over we hear tales, large and small, of the heart, the spirit, the soul reawakening to a greater vision of reality.

"It seems impossible that there is not a spiritual stream, a current of potential awakening that, when the moment is right, is waiting for each of us."[18]

We can each seek out and prepare ourselves for that moment. We can study the understandings and insights now emerging in the fields of both science and spirituality. Equipped with the new picture of reality on offer, we can practise stepping aside from our worries. We can develop

---

[18] *After the Ecstasy, the Laundry – How the Heart Grows Wise on the Spiritual Path,* Bantam Books, 2000

the power to remain stable, even in the midst of chaos.

With renewed awareness of the inner being, we become able to instruct the mind to let go, even briefly, of temporary everyday interests and concerns. Meditation enables us to bypass stress-filled thoughts, feelings, and perceptions that the brain puts before us, without recourse to drugs or austere religious practices.

As we recover our true sense of identity, as souls or "conscious agents", we loosen the hold of the limited ego. The more we die to the ego's demands for transient "kicks", pleasures, and short-lived success, the better our chances of restoring a sense of the peace, love, integrity, compassion and fulfilment that are intrinsic to the inner being.

Such "timeless treasures", Mother Julian of Norwich declared, are "always alive in us" – even though we may not have been alive to them. We are at our happiest when experiencing and expressing these profound qualities in our work and relationships, and seeing the same in the lives of others.

"The perfect you is the love within you," writes the American spiritual teacher Marianne Williamson.[19] "Closing our hearts destroys our peace. It's alien to our nature. Because thought is the creative level of things, changing our minds is the ultimate personal empowerment."

Both science and spirituality are showing us that the immortal soul is not just a belief or concept, but a truth to be realised and lived. Every human spirit begins its journey with this inheritance of strength and goodness – the attributes that make us most human. We don't have to try to become something we are not, but rather, to find ways of removing the accumulation of dust that prevents us from seeing clearly who we are.

Rumi, the 13th-century Islamic scholar and Sufi mystic, famously expressed this idea in saying that "Your task is not to seek love, but merely to seek and find all the barriers within yourself that you have built against it."

Hundreds of years later, that task still remains to be fulfilled.

---

[19] *A Return to Love, HarperCollins*, 1992

STEP SIX: THE FLAME

In the vastness of the universe, a flame of pure consciousness puts right that which has gone wrong

In *The God Theory*,[20] American astrophysicist Bernard Haisch offers an insight "into how you can, and should, be a rational, science-believing human being and at the same time know that you are also an immortal spiritual being, a spark of God."

This is not the punishing God so powerfully debunked by the Oxford evolutionary biologist Richard Dawkins, author of *The God Delusion*. Rather, an understanding of this One "offers a way out of the hate and fear-driven violence engulfing the planet," Haisch writes.

In his theory, an infinite, conscious intelligence – "so let's call it God" - pre-exists the universe. This intelligence has infinite potential, but it brings into being matter, energy, and the laws of nature in order to transform potential into actual experience.

---

[20] Weiser Books, 2006

He cites in support of his proposal the discovery in astrophysics that key properties of the Universe have just the right values to make life possible. He also describes how ancient mystical knowledge, exceptional human experiences, and cutting-edge science all point to a realm of purposeful light, an informational fabric, underlying what we see as the material universe.

Although the theory is not scientific proof, he says, it is capable of resolving some of the toughest problems the world faces. And it is compatible with the new science, and its revelation that "it is not matter that creates an illusion of consciousness, but consciousness that creates an illusion of matter".

In the Raja Yoga meditation taught by the Brahma Kumaris each of us is understood to have come from a place of pure potential, beyond space and time, where we reside with God, the Supreme Soul.

We are not God – but we can reconnect with God, and draw strength through that connection and relationship. It is a matter of remembering that pure One and our own divine origin, even while experiencing the physical realm.

In that loving union, we become renewed.

To consider ourselves to be God means to lose a vital distinction, between the pure consciousness that is the original basis of our humanity, and the limited consciousness in which many of us find ourselves today.

Raj Yogis live with the understanding that God has a specific role to play, when the suffering associated with loss of spiritual awareness becomes widespread and intense. The Supreme serves as a spiritual sun whose light of love and wisdom never fades; a reference point of what is highest in all of us.

Periodically, this light penetrates the shadows cast by our ignorance. When we meet this light, and open our hearts and minds to its Source, the darkness that caused us to lose sight of our highest nature is dispelled.

These are ancient understandings.

Teresa of Avila, a sixteenth-century Spanish nun and mystic, wrote: "Settle yourself in solitude and you will come upon God in yourself."

The Gospel of John, in the New Testament, declares "Dear friends, let us love one another, for love comes from God. Everyone who loves has been born of God and knows God. Whoever does not love does not know God because God is love."

Biblical statements of this kind refer to a transformative sense of relationship with the divine.

The theologian and author Rev. Dr Marcus Braybrooke, president of the World Congress of Faiths, sees prayer not just as a longing or asking, but as a way of connecting "like plugging in an electrical appliance or logging on to the Internet. We may not understand how electricity or the World Wide Web work, but we still benefit from using them," he writes in his valuable guide *Learn to Pray*[21].

"Likewise, when we pray we may not at first understand to whom we are praying, nor how we might be answered, but by daring to make the connection we can access a reservoir of energy and understanding that is buried within us."

For millennia, humanity drew comfort and inspiration from feelings and experiences of being uplifted by a divine

---

[21] Duncan Baird Publishers, London, 2001

intelligence, capable of guiding us at times of need.

Even in Western science, many of the greatest figures were deeply religious. Newton, Faraday, Maxwell, and the French mathematical genius Pascal, among others, were devout Christian thinkers. The strength they drew from their religious convictions helped them to push forward the boundaries of understanding of natural laws.

"We know the truth, not only by the reason, but also by the heart," Pascal wrote. He was also aware, however, that "Men never do evil so completely and cheerfully as when they do it from religious conviction."

Today, most of us, consciously and unconsciously, hold science in the highest regard because of the way it has helped advance our understanding of the world around us – and because of its attempts to free us from the evil to which ideology can give rise.

As knowledge and theory about the nature of the cosmos become more and more refined, however, time is calling us to let go of some of the familiar materialistic beliefs to which we have subscribed. This "letting go" is especially important in enabling us to better understand and empower ourselves.

According to the late John Wheeler, a highly regarded American theoretical physicist, "There may be no such thing as the 'glittering central mechanism of the universe' to be seen behind a glass wall at the end of the trail. No machinery but magic may be the better description of the treasure that is waiting."[22]

Einstein also showed an awareness of the limits of the scientific knowledge of his day. He wrote in a 1936 letter "Scientific research is based on the assumption that all events, including the actions of mankind, are determined by the laws of nature...On the other hand, however, everyone who is seriously engaged in the pursuit of science become convinced that the laws of nature manifest the existence of a spirit vastly superior to that of men, and one in the face of which we with our modest powers must feel humble."

Scholars from other disciplines are challenging some of science's traditional assumptions. Thomas Nagel, a distinguished philosopher, whilst acknowledging the value of the search for objective understanding, has highlighted the need for "a major conceptual revolution" to counter materialist dogma.[23]

---

[22] Quoted in *The Conscious Universe: The Scientific Truth of Psychic Phenomena*, by Dean Radin PhD (HarperOne, 2009)

[23] *Mind and Cosmos: Why the Materialist Neo-Darwinian Conception of Nature Is Almost Certainly False* (Oxford University Press, 2012)

Just as religion can degenerate into dogma and intolerance, science can do likewise when it becomes elevated into an ideology that labels spirituality as "anti-science".

Scientists take great pains to test theories, especially new ones, to try to avoid being fooled into believing something that is not true. However, as a wise philosopher has pointed out, there is a second way of being fooled, which is to refuse to believe what is true.

We have identified with the physical body and this material world for so long that we have forgotten who we truly are and what life on this earth is really about. Recognising our spiritual nature opens up a whole new world of possibilities and perspectives.

STEP SEVEN:
A STRANGE FREEDOM

*The outer world supports us in magical ways
when fear is overcome inside*

Could it be that in the depths of the human soul there is an unexplained force, an inner voice, capable of making a reality of the long-held dream of paradise?

Paradoxically, powerful confirmation of this idea comes from accounts of prisoners who suffered total deprivation in fearful punishment and labour camp conditions.

Aleksandr Solzhenitsyn tells in his three-volume *Gulag Archipelago* of how when you have nothing more to lose, a strange freedom emerges. "You only have power over people so long as you don't take everything away from them. But when you've robbed a man of everything, he's no longer in your power – he's free again", he writes. "Above all, don't cling to life. Possess nothing, free yourself from everything."

The freedom begins inside, not with thoughts but with an unshakeable set of inner values. Highly improbable "chance happenings" then enable those values to become manifest in the outer world.

"Each of us is the centre of the universe", Solzhenitsyn says foreshadowing the frontier science now telling us that the entire physical world is in some way linked to the depth of the soul.

The phenomenon is described in detail in *The Mystical Experience of Loss of Freedom*, an article written anonymously by "A Political Prisoner" more than 30 years ago. It was republished recently in the journal of the Scientific and Medical Network[24], an international forum founded in 1973 to reconcile scientific models of reality with the spiritual dimension of life.

The author draws on the works of Solzhenitsyn and three other former inmates of Soviet forced labour camps in giving us a picture that seems paradoxical.

"For instance, all the writers agree that arrest, imprisonment the camps, in short the loss of freedom are the most

[24] *Network Review,* 2016, Vol 3

important experiences of their lives. Moreover, they assure us that, although under these conditions they had to endure the worst forms of psychic and physical suffering, they experienced at the same time moments of utter happiness, such as those outside the camp walls could never imagine."

Still more remarkably, the writers "affirm unanimously that those who try to preserve their physical existence at the expense of their souls, lost both, while those who were prepared to sacrifice their bodies for the sake of their souls, by some mysterious law, and contrary to what they expected, had their physical existence preserved.

"This means that it is now an incontestable experience of life that in the depths of the human soul there swells an unexplained force which is stronger...than all outward forces of oppression and destruction, however invincible they may seem.

"Those who describe these happenings – which have been repeated and confirmed hundreds of times under the most frightful conditions of imprisonment – have come to the conclusion that powerful forms of psychic energy are dormant in every human soul...and that the thoughts and wishes of a person achieve far more in the outer, physical world than do his hands."

All four writers confirm that the body, "as they have seen again and again in themselves and others", responds with incredible toughness to strong spiritual concentration, while the loss of the spiritual leads to physical disintegration.

One who lets go of all outward trappings, decides to obey his inner voice, and discovers "this mysterious yet real force at work not only inside himself but in the outer world", realises at the same time that he is not master of this force, and cannot use it just as he might wish.

"On the contrary, he begins to understand that everything in his life, indeed life itself, is entirely dependent on the mysterious inner power, which, in the language of religion, is called God."

The article recounts a story told by Solzhenitsyn that illustrates "the mystical law of which we have been speaking".

"An astrophysicist in solitary confinement tried to avoid going mad by thinking out specific astrophysical laws and problems. At one point he could go no further because he did not know by heart some dates and figures he needed. The mental exercise which enabled him to keep sane, came to a full stop. In his despair he began to pray. He did not know as yet to whom, whether to God or an unknown power.

"A miracle happened. By mistake a textbook on astrophysics, which he could never have dreamt would be available in such a place, was brought to his cell from the prison library. When two days later the mistake was discovered and the book taken away again, the astrophysicist had already looked up and learned by heart all the dates he needed. His mental work could go on, and not only saved him but also helped him to discover a new theory...

"It was not the thought which had the effect. It was rather the mystical law, responding to a person's strong, inner concentration on a particular goal and bringing about the effect in an outside world seemingly beyond the person's influence." As Solzhenitsyn put it, "Heaven heard the prayers and intervened."

Strong, inner concentration on a particular goal sets off events in the outer world, which in turn set the stage for realising the inner goal. This finding "dynamites the idea forming the foundation of science," the article declares.

"At the same time, this inner striving is not voluntary It is not dependent on the desire or will of the person concerned. All that depends on the person is whether he wishes to follow the inner impulse or not...

"Man can hardly experience any greater happiness than the knowledge that he can influence events in the world against and in spite of the mighty influence of Evil. This freedom, born of obedience to the inner voice, the soul cannot be taken away from man by any outside force. He can only betray it himself."

STEP EIGHT: NEW POSSIBILITIES

*Can grace and integrity return to our world,
as we awaken to a greater vision of reality?*

Our journeys into inner space point us towards new possibilities in life. Once we recognise the power inherent in the spirit or soul – which is the true self – we can learn to take charge of our thoughts and feelings.

We discover what type of thoughts, feelings and actions lead us towards freedom, and what type keep us in chains. When we act against our highest nature, the treasures within become hidden. When we align ourselves with the soul's highest purpose, we retain our integrity, and become free.

Most of us are constantly confronted with inadequacies in ourselves and others. So we need to create in our everyday lives spaces where we step aside from those worries and concerns. When we do that, it becomes apparent that the treasures we most need are already within the soul.

What are those treasures? They lie within the peace the soul experiences when it has the fuller picture; the love it feels within divine relationship; and the bliss of pure being.

Physical aspects of existence demand our attention, especially in today's complex and uncertain world. But life can become stressful and joyless if we neglect the inner being, and let physical concerns take too strong a hold on our sense of who we are.

When that happens, we are bound to suffer, because everything in the physical world is temporary. That is in marked contrast to the soul and its journey, which lies within eternity.

It is as the eighteenth-century poet and artist William Blake wrote:

> *He who bends to himself a joy*
> *Doth the wingèd life destroy.*
> *But he who kisses the joy as it flies*
> *Lives in eternity's sunrise.*

For most of us, even when we recognise the wisdom of living lightly in this way, putting that into practice on a day by-day basis takes dedicated attention. This is because of conflicting drives acquired as a result of our mistaken identification with this physical world.

When we live with true self-awareness, we are free. In forgetting our spiritual identity, we allow our lives to become ruled by factors outside of ourselves.

When that happens, we feel insecure, and increasingly look to other people, situations and circumstances to take away our fears. We base our self-esteem on factors such as our job, talents, and physical appearance, constantly comparing ourselves with others.

These strategies give us a brief lift, a temporary feeling of being OK. This is why they become deeply established habits. But it is as if they take us half way across the river - and then drop us in it.

Disillusionment leaves its mark. Lack of self-esteem leads to critical and judgmental attitudes towards others. For many, it feels as if such tendencies are "part of our DNA".

Yet underneath all that, in our inner space, the truth never dies. We are eternal beings, and our true nature is of peace, love, and happiness.

"The Journey" we are sharing with you is intended to help you connect with that truth. We put it together in the hope of showing that the materialistic view of ourselves and life is an illusion; and that when we see past it, an inner freedom and lightness await us.

"Pure consciousness is a jewel of infinite beauty," writes the Oxford psychiatrist and psychotherapist Andrew Powell.

"We are no less indebted to the physical realm, for the gift of experience is infinitely precious too.

"Nevertheless, we carry great responsibility for what we do with our consciousness, since we can just as easily create hell as heaven.

"How may we give ourselves the best chance? While we have the inestimable gift of our individual identities within the bounds of space and time, in the quantum realm there is another truth to be discovered: that we are one. If humankind should ever learn that what belongs to one belongs to all, heaven on earth will be assured."[25]

---

[25] *The Ways of the Soul – A Psychiatrist Reflects,* Muswell Hill Press, London, 2017

As we return regularly to our own inner space, we develop the spiritual self-awareness that finishes negativity. Peace, love, courage, happiness and power flourish inside us. When such qualities, born of pure consciousness, are sufficiently restored in our minds, our world will transform.

For a thorn, the world is a thorn. For a flower, it is a flower!

JOURNEY INTO INNER SPACE

STEP NINE:
THE DESTINATION

A tiny star sparkles at the centre of a golden-red light. It represents the spiritual source of the highest in human consciousness.

As your final step in this introductory journey, you are invited to allow an experienced Raj Yogi to lead you towards the light of your own true being.

Zap the code on the image to hear a five-minute meditation on the soul led by Sister Jayanti, European and Middle East director of the Brahma Kumaris World Spiritual University (BKWSU).

ABOUT THE BRAHMA KUMARIS

The Brahma Kumaris is a network of organisations in over 100 countries, with its spiritual headquarters in Mount Abu Rajasthan, India.

It works at all levels of society for positive change, and offers individuals from all backgrounds a variety of life long learning opportunities to help them recognise their inherent qualities and abilities in order to make the most of their lives.

Acknowledging the intrinsic worth and goodness of the inner self, the Brahma Kumaris teaches a practical method of meditation, called Raja Yoga, that helps people to cultivate their inner strengths and values.

It also offers courses and seminars in such topics as positive thinking, overcoming anger, stress relief and self-esteem, encouraging spirituality in daily life.

This spiritual approach is also brought into healthcare, social work, education, prisons and other community settings.

All courses and activities are offered free of charge.

See the following page for contact details of the main offices.

For more information:
www.brahmakumaris.org

For more Brahma Kumaris publications:
www.inspiredstillness.com

E: hello@inspiredstillness.com

HOW AND WHERE
TO FIND OUT MORE

SPIRITUAL HEADQUARTERS

PO Box No 2, Mount Abu 307501,
Rajasthan, India
Tel: (+91) 2974-238261 to 68   Fax: (+91) 2974-238883
E-mail: abu@bkivv.org

INTERNATIONAL CO-ORDINATING OFFICE
& REGIONAL OFFICE FOR EUROPE
AND THE MIDDLE EAST

Global Co-operation House,
65-69 Pound Lane,
London, NW10 2HH, UK
Tel: (+44) 20-8727-3350   Fax: (+44) 20-8727-3351
E-mail: london@brahmakumaris.org

REGIONAL OFFICES

Please see next page...

REGIONAL OFFICES

AFRICA
Global Museum for a Better World,
Maua Close, off Parklands Road, Westlands
PO Box 123, Sarit Centre, Nairobi, Kenya
Tel: (+254) 20-374-3572   Fax: (+254) 20-374-3885
E-mail: nairobi@brahmakumaris.org

THE AMERICAS AND THE CARIBBEAN
Global Harmony House, 46 S. Middle Neck Road,
Great Neck, NY 11021, USA
Tel: (+1) 516-773-0971   Fax: (+1) 516-773-0976
E-mail: newyork@brahmakumaris.org

AUSTRALIA AND SOUTH EAST ASIA
181 First Ave, Five Dock,
Sydney, 2046
Australia
Tel: (+61) 2 9716-7066
E-mail: fivedock@au.brahmakumaris.org

RUSSIA, CIS AND THE BALTIC COUNTRIES
Brahma Kumaris World Spiritual University
2, Lobachika, Bldg. No. 2
Moscow – 107140

RUSSIA
Tel: (+7): +7499 2646276   Fax: (+7) 495-261-3224
E-mail: moscow@brahmakumaris.org